OFF TO ODISHA

SONIA MEHTA

PUFFIN BOOKS

An imprint of Penguin Random House

PUFFIN BOOKS

USA | Canada | UK | Ireland | Australia | New Zealand | India | South Africa | China | Singapore

Puffin Books is part of the Penguin Random House group of companies whose addresses can be found at global.penguinrandomhouse.com

Published by Penguin Random House India Pvt. Ltd
4th Floor, Capital Tower 1, MG Road,
Gurugram 122 002, Haryana, India

First published in Puffin Books by Penguin Random House India 2018

Text, design and illustrations copyright © Quadrum Solutions Pvt. Ltd 2018
Series copyright © Penguin Random House India 2018

Picture Credits

ISBN 9780143440987

Design and layout by Quadrum Solutions Pvt. Ltd

Printed at Repro India Limited

www.penguin.co.in

Hello Kids!

I'm so happy you are reading this book. India is an incredible country and there are lots of things about it that we never get to hear about.

I discovered India because my father was in the Indian army. He was posted to many places all over India—and we dutifully followed him. Can you imagine that by the time I was in the tenth standard, I had changed nine schools? Of course it was hard making new friends almost every year, but the good part was that I got to live in so many places. Right from Kerala, where I was born, to Kashmir, Jhansi, Shillong, Chandigarh, Goa . . . the list is long.

Every time I go to a new place, I feel amazed at how different each state is from the other—and yet, how similar. Did you know that we can see monuments from the Stone Age right here in India? Or that we have more than twenty official languages, and most Indians know three or four on an average? Or even that some of the world's most amazing scientific marvels were invented in India?

Oh, there are many, many, many fun and fantastic things about the states of India, which we simply must get to know.

So get your backpack ready, get set to meet some new friends and join me on a fun trip as we **DISCOVER INDIA, STATE BY STATE**.

I hope you enjoy reading this book as much as I have enjoyed writing it. I would love to hear from you. So do write to me at sonia.mehta@quadrumltd.com.

Lots of love,
Sonia Aunty

Mishki and Pushka have come to visit Earth from their home planet, Zoomba. They have never seen such an amazing place. Zoomba doesn't have trees and mountains and rivers like Earth does. But the people look exactly the same. When they come to Earth, they meet a sweet old man whom they call Daadu Dolma. Daadu Dolma shows them all the wonderful places in India and tells Mishki and Pushka all about them.

Mishki and Pushka can't believe what they see. They have seen a lot of Earth, but they have never, ever seen a place like India.

They are off to explore India state by state :)

Mishki

Mishki is a curious little girl. She is always asking loads of questions. On her home planet, she is always getting into trouble for poking her nose into things that are not her business.

Pushka

Pushka is Mishki's brother. He loves adventure. He is always ready to try a new challenge. Whether it's climbing a mountain, or diving into a cold, cold sea, he is up for it.

Daadu Dolma

Daadu Dolma is a wise old man who has lived on Earth longer than the mountains and seas. No one knows quite how old he is, but he certainly has been around. He knows everything about everything.

Mishki is all ready to leave. She is in a hurry to visit the next state. 'Daadu, where are we going this time?' she asks Daadu Dolma, jumping up and down.

'Stay still, Mishki,' Daadu replies, smiling. 'We are going to visit a beautiful state that is historical and very interesting.'

'Is the food yummy?' Pushka asks. Food is his one big love.

'Yes, the food is delicious and you are going to love it. But you will miss it all if you don't hurry,' Daadu tells them.

Pushka quickly packs his bag. Mishki is waiting impatiently. They are both excited to see a new state. They are

OFF TO ODISHA!!!

A SNEAK PEEK

Land ahoy!

That's right, Mishki. Odisha has different kinds of landforms, and it's lucky to have a bit of coastline as well. Come, let's explore.

Daadu, look! I can see a plateau. But I can also see the sea.

NEIGHBOURS ALL AROUND

Odisha is on the eastern shore of India. It has many friendly neighbours. Jharkhand, West Bengal, Andhra Pradesh, Telangana and Chhattisgarh are all its neighbours. The waters of the Bay of Bengal also lap its shores. So imagine how many borders it has.

For a long time, Odisha was known as Orissa.

ON THE MAP

To see exactly where Odisha is on the map of India, go to

http://www.mapsofindia.com/maps/india/india-political-map.htm

OLD, OLD LAND

The land of Odisha is very old. Some of the oldest rocks on Earth are found here. Imagine that! That must mean there were dinosaurs and other pre-historic beasts roaming this region at one time. But rocks are not all it has. There are ridges and plateaus that have been created by soil from rivers and sand blown in by the wind.

RIVERS APLENTY

There are some big and generous rivers in Odisha that keep the farms well irrigated. They have some long and lovely names. The Mahanadi, the Subarnarekha, the Budhabalanga, the Baitarani, the Brahmani, the Rushikulya and the Vamsadhara are some of them. Whew! Quite a mouthful to pronounce and remember!

FOREST FABLES

Odisha has loads of forests with many types of trees. The forests are deciduous (they shed their leaves every year). There are many kinds of trees in these forests, like teak, rosewood, bamboo and padauk.

You can just imagine how many lovely birds and animals must live in these forests.

JUST RIGHT!

The climate in Odisha is just right—not too hot and not too cold.
It's perfect tropical climate, though peak summer can get rather hot.
It rains from June to September, with the Eastern Ghats getting the most rain.

LOVELY LAGOON

Odisha also has one of India's largest saltwater lagoons, Chilka Lake. It is home to a whole lot of migratory birds, some wonderful underwater life and rare plants too! It even supports many fishermen, who make their living through this lake.

Ruddy shelduck at Chilka Lake

LOST IN THE LAKE

Pushka has lost his way while boating at the Chilka Lake. Can you help him find the right path to reach Daadu Dolma?

WONDERS OF THE WILD

The woodlands of Odisha are full of wonderful wildlife. The government has built many wildlife sanctuaries and parks, where animals are protected. Some of the large mammals you might see are many types of tigers, the four-horned antelope, gaurs (wild cattle), blackbucks and many species of monkeys.

A graceful crane at Chilka Lake.

FEATHERED FRIENDS

The best known bird you will see strutting around here is the gorgeous peacock. Around Chilka Lake, there are more than 150 species of birds that appear during the peak season between November and February. White-bellied sea eagles, ospreys, golden plovers, flamingos, shovelers and gulls are just some.

Some migratory birds that you find at Chilka Lake fly all the way from Iran, Siberia and Central Asia. Wow! What a distance to go!

KEEPING THEM SAFE

Many animals are kept safe in national parks. The Bhitarkanika Wildlife Sanctuary is said to be among Asia's finest. Do you know what's unique about it? It has many mangroves and a rich ecosystem. Spread across a vast area, this park has rivers, creeks, backwaters and mudflats that are home to wonderful creatures like the giant saltwater crocodile, king cobra, Indian python and water monitor lizards. Oooh! Exciting!

Saltwater crocodiles can look scary. Watch out!

FUN FACTS

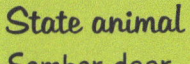
State animal
Sambar deer

State tree
Indian fig tree

State bird
Indian roller

State flower
Asoka

FLAMINGO FANTASY

Mishki and Pushka have both drawn flamingos. Can you spot five differences in the two pictures they have drawn?

11

CITY CITY BANG BANG

Odisha's cities are both historical and modern. Sounds confusing? Well, all it means is that many of these cities have a long and rich history. But they have modernized and now also have new infrastructure as well.

BHUBANESWAR

This is Odisha's capital city. It is an important cultural and historical city, full of ancient monuments. Its history can be traced all the way back to the third century BCE. You will see a blend of Hindu, Buddhist and Jain monuments. It has also been chosen to become one of India's Smart Cities due to its great infrastructure.

BERHAMPUR

One of Odisha's largest cities, it has been nicknamed the Silk City by some because it is famous for its silk saris. It also has many temples and a unique culture.

CUTTACK

Cuttack used to be the capital of Odisha at one time. Did you know that its name comes from the word *katak*, which means 'fort'? People also call Cuttack, the Millennium City, because it is said to be really old. Some call it the Silver City because it is famous for silver filigree work. It's now a busy industrial hub, but with loads of history tucked away.

SAMBALPUR

This city is a commercial and educational hub. It is well-known for the famous Sambalpuri sari. It also has the Hirakud Dam, one of the world's longest earthen dams.

ROURKELA

A super busy city, Rourkela is surrounded by hills and rivers. It is also known by some as Ispat Nagar (*ispat* means 'steel' in Hindi) because it has one of India's largest steel plants. It is yet another city that has been chosen to be a Smart City. It is also home to several small industries.

A workshop in a steel plant

PURI

This city is best known for its temples—the Shri Jagannath Dham being one of the most famous and important for Hindu pilgrims.

Long, long ago

Daadu, I can see a lot of really old monuments. That tells me that this place must have a long and interesting history. Am I right?

You certainly are. Odisha has a recorded history that is almost as old as India's history. And we all know that India is a really ancient civilization. Come, let's go into the past.

MANY NAMES

What we now call Odisha has had many names throughout history. It was called Utkala, Kalinga, Oddaka and Odra Desha in some of the oldest literature found. Some of these were the names of the tribes that lived in this region. The ancient Greeks wrote of tribes from this region—Kalingai and Oretes. These later came to be associated with specific regions.

Utkala
Kalinga
Oddaka
Odra Desha

ALREADY STRONG

The first written references of Indian history mention Kalinga as a strong and famous seat of power. King Brahmadatta was a famous Kalinga king, who lived during the time of Gautama Buddha. But his reign was not long, and his kingdom was soon under attack.

THE FIRST INDIAN DYNASTY

As far back as the fourth century BCE, one of India's first proper empires began to gain prominence, when a king called Mahapadma Nanda conquered Kalinga and established the Nanda Empire. But the Nanda rule didn't last long.

HERE COME THE MAURYAS

The great Mauryan emperor Ashoka, who was busy expanding his empire, invaded the Nanda Empire and fought a massive war, during which thousands of people were killed. Ashoka won the war but was so sad to see so much death and violence that he gave up war completely and became a Buddhist.

The Kalinga War is famous because it was after this war that Emperor Ashoka changed his ways and adopted Buddhism.

BACK COME THE KALINGAS

The Kalinga emperor Kharavela had been gathering his forces and wanted to get his ancestral kingdom back. He overthrew the Mauryas and expanded his kingdom. He made the Kalinga Empire strong again.

GOING ABROAD

The Kalinga Empire began to spread not only in a large part of India but also went overseas. It had a strong navy, and people believe that it established an empire called the Shailendra Empire in the island of Java (now in Indonesia). It is believed that they also colonized parts of Sri Lanka, Bali, Sumatra, Thailand and Vietnam.

A monument in Indonesia from the times of the Shailendra Empire

No wonder many of these countries have so many cultural similarities with India. Their literature even has references to epics like the Ramayana and the Mahabharata.

MANY KALINGA DYNASTIES

Many dynasties ruled the region of Kalinga, each adding their own special touch. The Somas, the Suryas, the Vasishthas, the Matharas, the Pitrbhaktas and the Gangas were some. The Kalinga Empire is supposed to have had a Golden Age under the Gangas, during which the people and the land prospered.

Coins from the Eastern Ganga Dynasty

Akbar was a strong Mughal king.

The Ganga rulers were the ones who built the world-renowned Shri Jagannath temple at Puri and the Sun Temple at Konark.

MIGHTY MUGHALS

For several hundred years, the region of Odisha was disorganized after the Kalinga Empire became weak, with no strong king at the helm. The Afghans ruled for a while. Around this time, the mighty Mughals, under Emperor Akbar, grabbed Odisha and established themselves. They successfully ruled over this region for many years.

RHYME AWAY

Mishki wants to make up a poem about the kings who ruled Odisha. She needs to find words that rhyme with STRONG. Can you help her find at least five rhyming words?

STRONG

_____ _____

_____ _____

_____

THE MARATHAS WERE HERE

The Marathas had become strong under King Shivaji. They conquered the central part of Odisha while the north and south was taken over by the Nizam of Hyderabad and the nawab of Bengal. Imagine how fragmented the region was!

A Maratha warrior

BRITISH BOOM

The British spotted India as a wonderful place to expand their empire. They began as traders but soon fought battles with the Indian kings and made India a British colony. A massive battle between the Indians and the British, the Battle of Plassey, brought a large part of eastern India—including Odisha and West Bengal—under British control.

UNITED BY LANGUAGE

India is a huge country. To make it easier to manage, the British organized the country into different regions. The people who spoke Oriya (the language of Odisha) fought hard to be united. Finally, the British agreed and brought together all the regions in which people spoke Oriya into a separate province.

How interesting all this is!

SO UNFAIR

The British made many laws that were unfair to the Indians. The Indians were furious; they wanted their independence. Many battles ensued between the Indians and the British.

The Independence struggle is one of the most important events in Indian history.

INDEPENDENCE AT LAST

Finally, in 1947, India became independent. But even then, Odisha was not the state that it is today. Many parts of today's Odisha belonged to other regions. It was in 1950 that Odisha was declared a proper Indian state, made up of the people who spoke Oriya—the local language.

WHAT'S ODD?

In every row, there's one word that's odd. Can you circle it?

SOMA	SURYA	ROMAN	VASHISHTA

MARATHA	GREEK	KALINGA	MUGHAL

ORIYA	MARATHI	FRENCH	GUJARATI

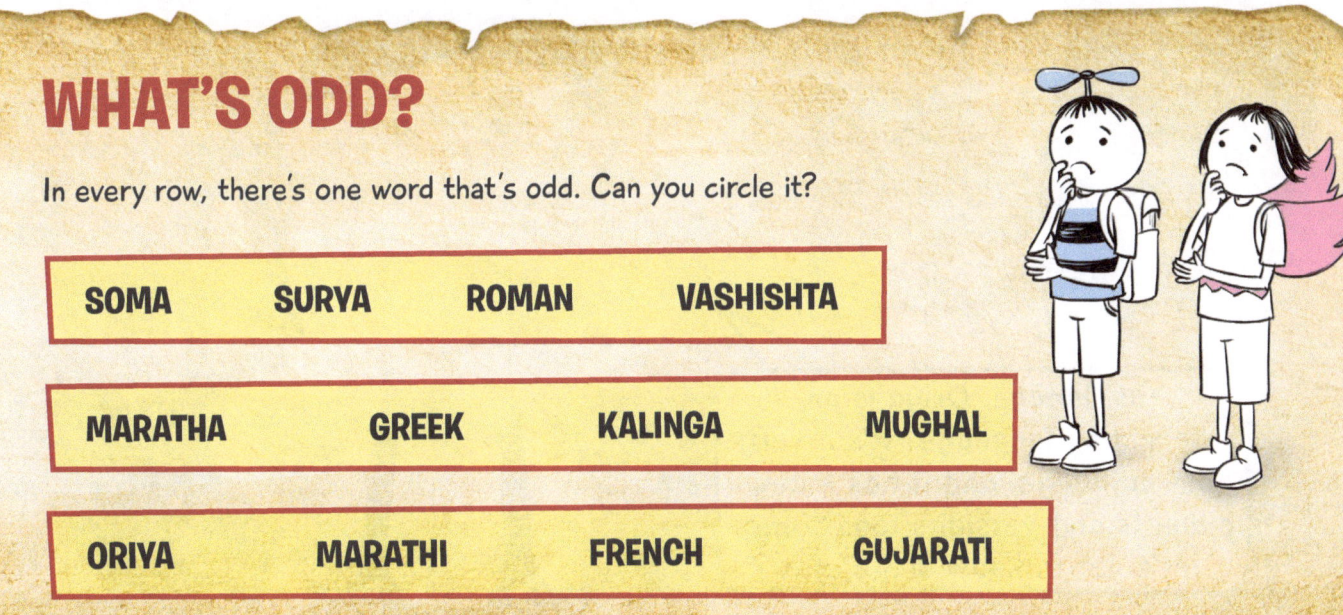

Talk time

Wow! That was amazing. Now I would love to know more about the language, Daadu, so I can speak to people here.

Yes, indeed. Oriya is an interesting language. It's a very old language, and it has many dialects and versions too. Come, let's get to know some of it.

Oriya (also called Odia) is so old that the first time we see it in use is almost a thousand years ago. It even has its own script, which is similar to the Bengali script. People used to write it on palm leaves with an iron nib.

- Welcome = Swaagoto
- Hello = Nomoscar
- Sorry = Khema koro
- Thank you = Dhanyabad
- Please = Doyakaro

- How are you? = Aapono kemiti achonti?
- What is your name? = Tamoro na kono?
- My name is Mishki = Moro na Mishkio
- Bon appetit (enjoy your meal) = Subh trupti
- Do you speak Oriya? = Aapono Oriya kotha kohonti?
- Good Morning = Suprabhat
- Goodbye = Bideyo

Did you know?
A lot of people in Odisha also speak Bangla.

WORD MATCH

Match the English words to their Oriya meanings. Pushka seems to have already forgotten!

| Hello | Thank you | Sorry | Please | How are you? | Goodbye |

| Bideyo | Aapono kemiti achonti? | Doyakaro | Nomoscar | Khema koro | Dhanyabad |

A peep into their life

This is very cool, Daadu. I can now talk to the people in Odisha. But what kind of people are they? I'd love to know about their lives.

Odisha has a colourful lot of people. The festivals, dances and music are all very lovely. We can start by learning about the people first.

TRIBAL TRACT

It is said that Odisha has among the greatest number and types of tribes in India. They are what make the culture so colourful. Some of these tribes live in rather isolated areas, and their lifestyle is still very simple. The Bondas and Odishan are two such simple tribes. They hunt, farm, eat off the land and live in tiny communities. But others have merged into modern life, bringing with them their music, dance and festivals.

The tribes of Odisha have lovely names. Santhal, Savara, Juang, Khond, Gond, Oraon and Bhuiyan are some.

22

A MIX OF RELIGIONS

Though Hindus make up the largest number of people in this state, there are great numbers of Muslims, Christians and Buddhists too. The various temples, mosques and churches here are proof of this.

TRIBAL TWINS

Mishki has made copies of a tribal painting but only two are exactly alike. Can you find those two?

A

B

C

D

A DANCE THAT'S A CLASSIC

Perhaps one of India's most famous dance forms, Odissi is a classical one—and just as its name suggests, it was born here. In the olden days, women would perform this dance for the entertainment of gods—or so they believed. These women were called *devdasis*. The dance they performed evolved into the Odissi dance.

FOLK DANCES GALORE

With so many tribes and so many rural people, the folk dances of Odisha are lovely. There are just too many for us to see them all, but here are some really colourful ones.

RANAPA DANCE

Ranapa means 'stilts', and (as the name suggests) this dance is performed on stilts. The dancers perform skilfully to the beat of dhol (a kind of drum) and a *mahuri* (a wind instrument).

> I am going to try this step out for sure.

KARMA DANCE

This energetic dance is performed by the tribal people of Odisha, as well as some from other states. Every autumn, people perform a massive puja called Karma Puja. They pray to a tree called the Karam tree, a symbol of the god of prosperity. The dancers—both men and women—dance around the tree to the beat of drums called *timki*.

GHOOMRA

The *ghoomra* is a drum that is shaped like a huge pitcher. Its face is made of reptile skin (eeks!) and it makes a resounding boom when struck. It is to this beat that the ghoomra dancers perform. Fifteen days before a full moon night in September, they collect and do this dance every night. They sing songs in praise of God and do this joyous dance.

DALKHAI

This dance gets its name from the fact that at the start and end of every verse, performers use the word *dalkhai*, which is a way of addressing one's girlfriend. It depicts the love story of Radha and Krishna.

CHHAU

This famous dance is shared by some other states as well! In the past, only men were allowed to do this; now, women take part too! It is believed to have originally been a war dance. The dancers wear magnificent masks and perform to the beat of a kettle drum called a *dhumusa*. Within *chhau* too there are different forms of dance, all of which are fun to see and do!

25

FESTIVAL FRENZY

Ah, the festivals! Odisha is full of charming, exciting and vibrant festivals. There are religious festivals, cultural festivals, music festivals and dance festivals. There is always a reason to celebrate.

BASELI PUJA

This is a festival celebrated by fisherfolk. They pray to a god called Baseli—a deity with the head of a horse. A dummy horse head is created. For an entire month, devotees pray, ending each prayer with a frenetic dance. At the end of the month, the horse head is restored to the temple, where it stays all year.

KONARK DANCE FESTIVAL

This is a colourful event where people celebrate the different dance forms of India. It is held against the backdrop of the stunning Sun Temple in Konark. Dancers from all over India come and perform here, and people from all over the world come to enjoy and appreciate dance.

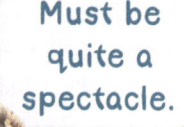

Must be quite a spectacle.

JAGANNATH TEMPLE FESTIVALS

Ratha Yatra

There are numerous festivals held at the Shri Jagannath Temple in Puri all through the year, during which people pray to Lord Jagannath. Devotees come from across India (and even overseas) for some of these festivals. Here are two of the most famous.

Ratha Yatra, where decorated idols of Lord Jagannath are placed on massive chariots and taken around in a procession.

Chandan Yatra, where people celebrate and pray on decorated floating *rathas* at night.

Chandan Yatra

WHAT'S THE WORD?

Help Mishki solve all the clues and then find the hidden word in the blue squares!

Clues

1. The word they start and end with during this performance

2. The dance during which people pray to a tree

3. A dance on stilts

4. A dance wearing masks

5. The ghoomra drum is made of this skin

Bricks and stones

I think I would be happy to live in Odisha forever. But if I did, what kind of house would I live in, Daadu?

Well, Mishki, it depends on where in Odisha you would live. You see, tribal houses are very different from those in cities. Let's see what kind of homes people build in Odisha.

TRIBAL STYLE

Many tribes in Odisha live in small, happy communities. They even have dormitories in which younger people live. A tribe called the Juangs have the most organized system. In the centre of this community's village is the largest hut. It has walls on three sides and is open in the front. The walls are decorated with patterns. The village elders collect here to discuss important matters and celebrate festivals and events.

ALL IN ONE

Many village houses have a space for everything they need. Typically, each house has a common veranda. It even has a small room for cattle. The rooms are usually arranged around a courtyard, which is a very important part of the house because it's here that families and friends hang out. People also cook in the courtyard. Sometimes, there is a huge backyard called a *bari*, where cut paddy is stored.

A bari in a rural house in Odisha

IN TUNE WITH MOTHER NATURE

Houses here are built to withstand the fury of cyclones, keeping the people safe.

In villages here, houses are built to suit the climate. People use local materials that are easily available. Walls are made of mud or stone, and roofs are thatched. Some advanced homes have *attu* roofs. Attu is a mud ceiling with bamboo or timber rafters. Want to know something special? The material ensures that hot air is forced out, keeping the house cool in summer. Isn't that clever?

COLOURFUL JOY

The people of Odisha are really colourful. That's why they like colour in their homes too. When you go into small towns, you will see houses painted in bright colours, especially in a small town called Raghurajpur, where lots of craftsmen live. The houses here are a visual treat with bright walls and lovely patterns too.

Standing strong

Daadu, I have slept well and am ready to see some interesting monuments. Are there any in Odisha?

Pushka, if you are in the mood to see monuments, you have come to the right place. Odisha has some of India's most beautiful structures.

TEMPLE BELLS

Some of India's most amazing temples are in Odisha. That is because its various kings were great lovers of architecture and constructed many wonderful temples.

THE SUN TEMPLE

Also known as the Konark Sun Temple, this was built by a king called Narasimhadeva thousands of years ago. It is designed to look like the giant chariot that carries Surya (the sun god) across the heavens. A part of the temple is in ruins and sits in the middle of shifting sand. There are carved figures of horses and elephants that help you imagine the chariot being pulled by them across the sky.

In the past, European sailors used this temple as a guiding point when they navigated their ships to shore. They called it the Black Pagoda.

THE JAGANNATH TEMPLE

People from all over the world come to visit this magnificent temple in Puri. A ruler from the Eastern Ganga dynasty built this temple thousands of years ago. There are three deities that are worshipped here—Jagannath, Balabhadra and Subhadra.

CHAUSATHI YOGINI TEMPLE

Here is a temple with a difference. It has the idols of sixty-four goddesses called yoginis. Wow! That's a lot of deities in one temple. People believe that every village has a mascot goddess that looks after the village. The temple has a specific niche for each yogini idol. Wouldn't you love to see this amazing temple that is so very old?

THE RAJARANI TEMPLE

Rajarani means 'king–queen'. But that's not what the temple is named after. It is, in fact, named after the type of stone with which it has been built. The name of the stone is rajarani! This temple has not just deities but also beautiful carvings of people—like a mother with her baby, a woman looking into a mirror and people playing musical instruments.

Isn't that unusual in a temple?

31

ON THE TRAIL OF THE BUDDHA

Emperor Ashoka spread a lot of the Buddha's teachings in the region that was Odisha. Many kings who came after him supported Buddhism too, and they allowed people to build monuments to honour Gautama Buddha. There are three famous Buddhist complexes. They are called the Diamond Triangle. Let's see all of them.

A VAST MONASTERY

Archaeologists were thrilled to discover a huge complex of Buddhist monasteries in a place called Udayagiri. You can imagine Buddhist monks praying, meditating and living here hundreds of years ago. There are monasteries made of brick, a stepped-stone well from where the monks collected water and a stupa too! Even though a lot of it is in ruins, this is a beautiful place to get a glimpse of the past.

A MONASTERY AND A MUSEUM

Lalitgiri is another corner of the Diamond Triangle. It's here that there have been discoveries of not only many amazing stupas and monasteries but also statues, inscriptions on tablets, stone caskets with Buddhist icons, and gold and silver jewellery. In fact, the findings are so amazing that there is now a museum where you can go and see these artefacts. Wow!

A UNIVERSITY OF BUDDHIST LEARNING

In a place called Ratnagiri (not the one in Maharashtra), there is a huge collection of Buddhist remains. Some years ago, archaeologists decided to dig deep and, to their delight, found Buddhist shrines, sculptures, stupas and monasteries. This place is so well-known that it has even been mentioned in Tibetan Buddhist texts by Tibetan scholars.

SPOT THE DIFFERENCE

Look at these two lovely pictures of the Buddha meditating. Can you find five differences between them?

TWIN WONDERS

Very close to the capital city, Bhubaneshwar, stand the twin hills of Khandagiri and Udayagiri. These hills are a treasure trove of historical monuments. The rocks of these hills were cut, carved and tunnelled into to make cosy residences for Jain monks.

A ROYAL DREAM

King Kharavela, who did a lot to expand the Kalinga kingdom, was a wise man and a visionary. He made sure there were canals to irrigate his kingdom and that there was law and order in his land. He began the process of carving the Khandagiri Caves for the convenience of Jain monks. His queen also felt strongly about things of beauty, and she had a lot to do with the beautiful carvings you see here.

Imagine how long it must have taken!

THE QUEEN'S CAVE

There is a famous cave called Rani Gumpha in Udayagiri. This even has an upper and a lower storey, and a beautiful courtyard. There are magnificent carvings on the walls that depict legends, dancers and musicians too! The queen must have loved her home.

What an amazing place to live in!

CAVERNOUS SIGHTS

There are a large number of caves in these twin hills. One of them is the famous Hathigumpha (Elephant Cave) in Udayagiri. The many inscriptions on these caves tell us about King Kharavela's military conquests; they describe the city, its bathing and water tanks, its gateways, and its entertainment and sporting halls. We can imagine what life was like in those days.

THE GANESHA GUMPHA

This is close to the Rani Gumpha and was in all likelihood its extension at one time. This lovely cave has an elephant sculpture right up front. There are incredible carvings of warriors, gods, kings and queens. This certainly tells you that the people of this state have always been super creative and imaginative.

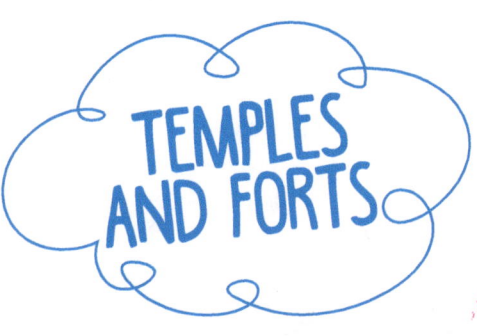

TEMPLES AND FORTS

A TANK WITH A STORY

Bindusagar Tank, a lovely lake with a temple in the middle of it, has a story behind it. Lord Shiva and Parvati came here after they got married. Shiva wanted to meditate so he disguised himself. Parvati went searching for him. After a while, she grew tired and thirsty. When Shiva saw this, he struck his trident into the ground and a spring emerged from it. This is what people believe is Bindusagar Tank.

What a lovely story!

THE BARABATI FORT

This really ancient fort was built by the kings of the Ganga dynasty hundreds of years ago. Even though most of it is sadly in ruins, the remains of a nine-storeyed palace are still clearly visible. There is a moat and a gateway too.

Can't you imagine horses galloping through?

BRINGING THE RAMAYANA TO LIFE

Sitabhinjh is where people say Sita lived in exile and where she gave birth to her twin sons—Luv and Kush. There is a river named the Sita that flows close by. The hills surrounding this area are named after characters from the Ramayana—Valmiki, Luv, Kush, Surpanakha and Ravana. Imagine that! It's like walking into the pages of the Ramayana.

In honour of Sita

VISHNU IN ROCK

On the banks of the Brahmani River lies a massive sculpture of Lord Vishnu that is carved on a flat rock. People say this is one of the world's largest horizontal rock carvings. It is said to be more than fifty feet long. People come from all over the world to see this amazing sight.

HIDDEN WORDS

Sitabhinjh is such a long name. Can you make eight smaller words from it? Mishki has made one.

SITABHINJH

SIT

_____ _____ _____

_____ _____

_____ _____

CHUDANGAGARH FORT

King Chodagandadeva of the Ganga dynasty decided to build a fort to safeguard his massive empire. He built Chudangagarh Fort, complete with temples, water tanks, a large palace, a granary and watchtowers. People could live here and stay safe in this fort during enemy onslaughts.

ASURGARH FORT

Asurgarh Fort was a massive and imposing structure at one time. With walls that were thicker than the width of a room and a wide moat all around, it must have been impossible for enemies to enter. Asurgarh was one of the earliest towns, and it is said that the people who lived here were cultured and educated. Now, the fort is in ruins, but you can imagine what it used to be like.

The lion has become a symbol of Emperor Ashoka.

THE SITE OF A FIERCE BATTLE

The famous Kalinga War, after which Emperor Ashoka gave up fighting, was fought at a place called Dhauli. Legend says that the battle was so fierce that the river turned red with blood. When King Ashoka turned to Buddhism, he made sure that he built stupas, pillars and residences for Buddhist monks. Dhauli became an important place for Buddhists.

CRAZY CROSSWORD

Can you solve this crossword for Mishki and Pushka? They seem to be stuck.

ACROSS

3. Another word for cave that starts with the letter 'G'.

4. King Kharavela carved hills for the comfort of Jain _____.

6. Lalitgiri has a _____ where you can see amazing artefacts.

7. A city where you can see Buddhist remains. It rhymes with Lalitgiri.

DOWN

1. The Buddhist complexes make up the _____ Triangle.

2. Caves were carved in these for Jain monks to live in.

3. An elephant god.

Working hard

Well, you will need to work too! How about discovering what the people in Odisha do for a living? So you can decide what kind of work you would like to do when you're older!

Okay, now I am definitely ready to settle down in Odisha. I will spend all my time sightseeing.

FISHING AWAY

Because Odisha has a long coastline as well as many lakes, lagoons and swamps, fishing is a fairly important occupation. There are many fishermen who catch both saltwater and seawater fish!

FACTORY FRENZY

There are many factories in Odisha that produce all kinds of things: cement, glass, fertilizers, chemicals, tyres and much more. All these are called heavy industries. Working in a factory can be hard work.

HEAVY METAL

Odisha's soil is rich in minerals, like manganese ore, graphite, chromite, bauxite and coal. This state is also one of India's largest producers of iron ore. There are many iron and steel mines here, where people work hard to mine these metals.

ON THE FARM

Odisha has a lot of land that is not too fertile. In spite of that, there are a large number of farmers. They grow many things, like rice, pearl millet, sugar cane, coconut and spices. But because the land is so hard to till, many farmers need to add to their income by having other jobs. Sometimes, family members work in factories to help out.

HANDY HANDICRAFT

Odisha was once called Utkala (like in India's national anthem), which means 'the land of wonderful art'. No wonder that the people of Odisha are so skilled in making beautiful things. Let's see what designs and art these people create.

PATTACHITRA ARTISTS

This means 'painting on cloth'. The artists who do this work are very talented and paint the most amazing scenes on silk. People also used to make circular playing cards using this style.

PERFECT PIPLI

The various tribes of Odisha have developed this art form that the state is now famous for. It is a kind of applique called *pipli*. Artists cut pieces of cloth in different animal, bird or flower shapes. They then attach these to larger pieces of cloth to make umbrellas and wall hangings. This is named after the village of Pipli, where this art form originated.

What beautiful and intricate patterns! You must need a lot of skill to create these.

Sari from Odisha

WEAVING MAGIC

The weavers of Odisha are world-famous for the lovely weaves they create. Odisha is known for its special saris. They have names like *khandua*, *saktapda*, *bomkai* and *tarabali*.

I want to wear that sari.

BRASS BONANZA

The artists who create these wonderful brass pieces are called *kansaris*. They make amazing objects by beating brass, then heating it in a furnace and shaping it. It's a complicated process that many of these craftsmen have been doing for generations.

TYRED

Look at these tyres made in a factory. Can you find two that are identical?

A   B   C   D   E

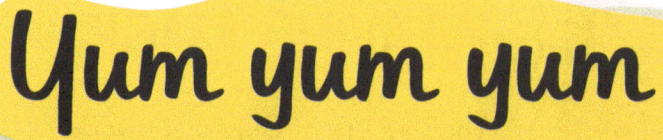

Yum yum yum

Daadu, I bet Pushka is really hungry by now, so where are you taking him?

I am taking both of you on a food trip you will never forget.

BELA PANA

This cool drink is a mix of fruit, coconut milk, curd, spices—and guess what! Yummy rasagullas are also crushed and added to this drink. It is made during festivals, including the Odiya new year. People also believe it's great for sunstroke and tummy upsets. **Mmmmm!**

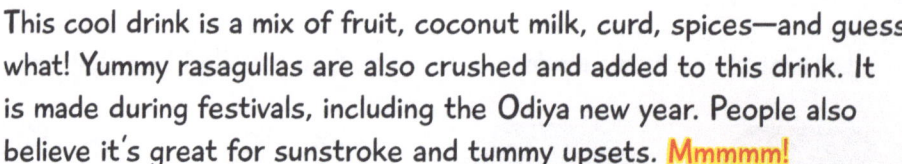

LOVELY LAU KHIRSA

This delicious (and healthy) dish is eaten for breakfast. It's a porridge made of rice, gourd and milk. It's sweet and most satisfying as a day starter.

BHAJA DELIGHT

Bhaja means 'fried'. Odiya people make many dishes by frying different vegetables and meats.

POKHALO PERFECTION

Pokhalo bhato is essentially a rice dish—with variations. Basi pokhalo is a version in which the rice is fermented overnight. Saja pokhalo is similar but eaten when it's just made. It's a healthy dish that people have with green chillies, onions and yoghurt!

DELICIOUS DALMA

This dish is made with lentils and vegetables. People put in many kinds of veggies, like green papaya, eggplant, pumpkin and raw banana. Sounds healthy, all right!

MACHA BESARA

A lot of Odiya food is similar to that of West Bengal. Like their Bangla neighbours, here too people love their fish and add mustard to their cooking. Macha besara is an example. This is a delicious fish curry that is made with plenty of mustard paste.

KHIRA GAINTHA

You have to try this pudding that is made of rice, milk, coconut and sugar. It's simply delicious!

YUMMY KHOJA

Khoja is a deep fried dumpling that's a little sweet and a little salty. It tastes like heaven.

CHINGUDI TARKARI

This dish is a mix of prawns and vegetables. It is a delicious curry that tastes terrific with rice.

KHIRA PODA PITHA

An absolute must if you like sweets like Pushka does. These are little pudding squares made of rice, milk and sugar. They taste as nice as they look.

Yummmmy!

HEALTHY SALAD

Mishki wants to make a healthy salad. Can you circle all the vegetables for her and leave the fruit out?

What to wear?

Daadu, we are very full now. I want to wear something nice and comfy. What kind of clothes will I get in Odisha?

Oh, there's a large variety. Colourful tribal clothes, traditional costumes and, of course, modern outfits. You have a lot to choose from!

TRIBAL DRESS SENSE

There are as many traditions as there are tribes. Some tribes wear different clothes for different occasions. And some have different styles for different people. In one tribe, unmarried girls wear fine clothes to attract husbands, while priestesses wear heavy formal clothes for prayer.

Many tribes even weave the cloth for their clothes. How's that for DIY!

DIFFERENT STYLES

Some tribes, who live in isolation and away from civilization, simply drape a cloth around themselves. Men and women have similar outfits. But some tribes have modernized: women wear short saris and men wear dhotis. Tribal women wear elaborate headgear and jewellery too!

In some tribes, both men and women have elaborate tattoos all over their bodies. Ouch. Must hurt!

CITY DWELLERS

In the towns and cities, people have a fairly modern way of dressing. Women often wear the handloom saris that Odisha is so famous for. Men wear dhoti—kurtas with a cloth called a *gamucha* thrown over their shoulders. Many prefer being comfortable in pyjamas.

SOMETHING'S ODD

In each row, there is something odd. Can you circle the odd word?

| Sari | Skirt | Dhoti | Gumboots |

| Jeans | T-Shirt | Cloak | Trousers |

| Bangle | Nose ring | Anklet | Rubber band |

Autograph, please?

I am all ready with my autograph book to meet some famous people. Who are we going to meet?

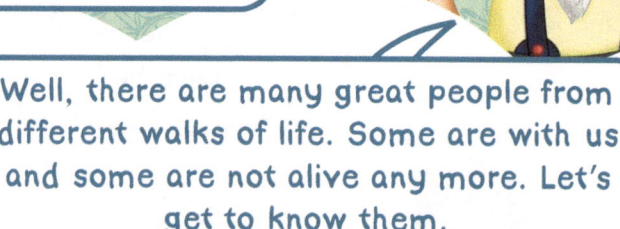

Well, there are many great people from different walks of life. Some are with us and some are not alive any more. Let's get to know them.

FAKIR MOHAN SENAPATI

He was a great poet, who wrote amazing poetry in pure Oriya. People call him the father of Oriya literature. He was one of the people who helped give Odisha its own special identity.

SARALA DAS

He was one of Odisha's earliest poets, who lived in the fifteenth century CE. He wrote three books that became really famous—the Mahabharata (in Oriya), *Vilanka Ramayana* and *Chandi Purana*. He was one of the first to write in Oriya.

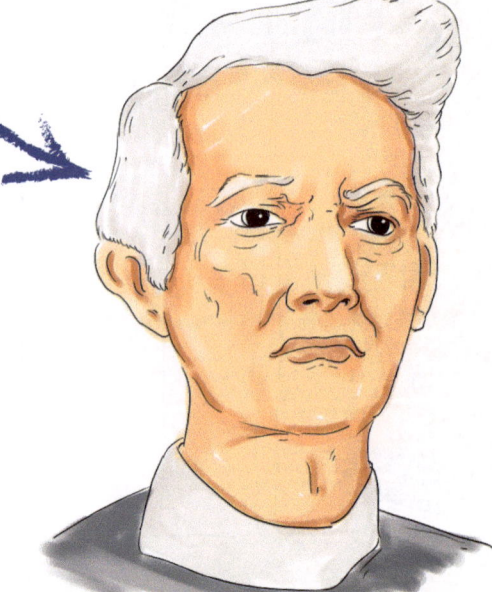

CHAITANYA MAHAPRABHU

Chaitanya Mahaprabhu was a Hindu mystic and a Bhakti saint, whose teachings influenced people in Odisha and Bengal. Though he was born in a small village in Bengal, he spent twenty-four years of his life in Puri. He used a form of worship called *kirtana*, which involved singing hymns and dancing. Chaitanya Mahaprabhu has a huge following in Odisha even now.

GURU KELUCHARAN MOHAPATRA

He was an Indian classical dancer and great Odissi master. All his life, he taught dance and worked hard to spread the popularity of Indian classical dance forms. He was awarded the Padma Vibhushan.

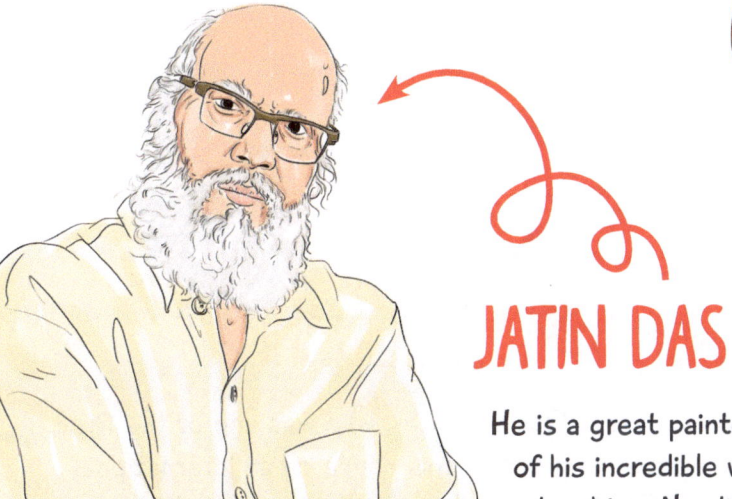

JATIN DAS

He is a great painter and sculptor, who has held exhibitions of his incredible work all over India and abroad too! His daughter, Nandita Das, is a well-known actor.

BIBHU MOHAPATRA

Born in Rourkela, Bibhu Mohapatra is an internationally renowned fashion designer. Though he lives in New York, he has designed a collection to help traditional Odiya weavers. He has dressed many famous women around the world.

SUDARSHAN PATTNAIK

He is a world-famous sand artist. His sand sculptures are breathtaking. He was awarded the Padma Shri for his amazing talent.

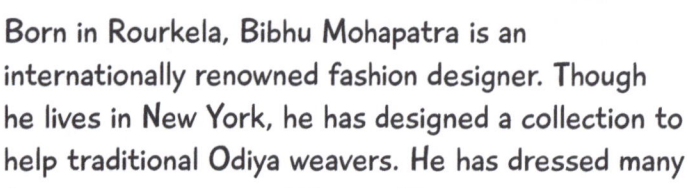

SANJUKTA PANIGRAHI

She was a great Odissi dancer, who was one of the first Odiya women to perform this dance on an international platform. She has won many awards for her brilliant work.

DR RAMAKANTA PANDA

He is a great heart surgeon, who has performed thousands of high-risk surgeries and saved so many lives. He is believed to be among the best surgeons in the world in his specialization.

PADMINI ROUT

She is a chess player who has won titles like International Grandmaster and Woman Grandmaster. She began early and even won the World Under 14 Girls championship. She has won many national chess tournaments.

MATCH THEM RIGHT

Match the personality with what they are known for.

Padmini Rout	Sanjukta Panigrahi	Jatin Das	Dr Ramakanta Panda

Odissi dancer	Heart surgeon	Chess player	Painter

Once upon a time . . .

That was impressive, Daadu. I like Odisha. But I'm tired! Can we sit somewhere while you tell us a story?

Most certainly. Come, I will tell you a folk tale from the state of Odisha.

THE SUSPICIOUS MERCHANT

Gopala was a wealthy merchant who lived in a small town in Odisha. He had everything he needed. But the one thing he didn't have was belief. He was suspicious of everybody.

If his friends told him that it was going to rain, he didn't believe them. 'You are simply saying so because you don't want me to step out of my house. You must be planning something without me,' he would say.

If his wife told him that there was no fish in the house, he would snap at her and say, 'I don't believe you. You are simply saying that because you can't be bothered to cook for me.'

Everyone was fed up of Gopala and his suspicious ways.

'One day, you will learn a lesson,' his friends would say.
But Gopala would simply scoff at them.

One afternoon, when Gopala was returning home from work, he saw a man on the beach. The man was dressed oddly and doing something very strange. He was painstakingly scooping up cupfuls of sand and pouring it on to a mound. With every cup he poured, the mound grew.

Gopala watched him for a while, intrigued by what he was doing. Finally, his curiosity got the better of him.

'Who are you, and what are you doing?' he asked the man.

'My name is Bidhata. I am fate,' the man replied.

'Fate is not a man,' scoffed Gopala. 'What are you collecting sand for?' he demanded. As usual, he was suspicious.

'Well, I am measuring out the amount of food everyone will get to eat today,' the man explained. 'If I miss even one person's quota, that person will go hungry.'

At this, Gopala started laughing.

'Oh, you silly man,' he snorted. 'My wife cooks my food. Do you mean to tell me that if you don't measure out a cup of sand for me, I will go hungry today?'

'That is so,' the man agreed.

'Ha ha ha,' Gopala laughed. 'Well, then, I challenge you. Don't scoop up my share, and you will see that I'll still eat a full meal.'

The man smiled and agreed. Gopala walked off home, still laughing loudly.

When Gopala reached home, he was still laughing.

His wife had made a delicious meal of fish curry and rice. She placed it in front of him. Gopala was still thinking of his encounter with the strange man.

What a foolish man to think he can control my food, Gopala thought. *See, I am about to eat my lunch.* He found the idea so funny that he began to laugh again. He laughed so much that he couldn't speak at all.

'What is the matter with you?' his wife snapped.

'My l . . . l . . . lunch,' gasped Gopala, still guffawing.

'You find the food I have cooked funny?' his wife demanded angrily. 'Wait, I will teach you a lesson.' She snatched away the plate of food and stomped into the kitchen. She shut the kitchen door and sat down.

'Let him go hungry,' she said to herself. 'That will teach him to laugh at my food.'

Gopala banged hard on the kitchen door.

'Open the door, woman!' he yelled, looking in through the window. But his wife was so angry she refused to open the door.

The afternoon turned to evening, and Gopala got no lunch. Bidhata certainly seemed to have made sure that he got no food.

From that day on, Gopala stopped being so suspicious and began to believe what people said, even though it was sometimes quite unbelievable.

TRAVEL DIARY

Have you enjoyed this trip to Odisha with your friends Mishki and Pushka—and, of course, with Daadu Dolma?

Now you can make your own Odisha diary. And if you ever visit Odisha, make sure you take pictures and put them in the photo box.

The first place I would visit in Odisha:

_____

If I could perform one of the folk dances, I would perform:

_____

The one dish I am definitely going to eat:

_____

The monument I think is the most interesting:

_____

The one famous person from Odisha I would love to meet:

_____

I think the most interesting historical figure from Odisha is:

_____

The festival from Odisha that I think is the most fun:

_____

The five words that I think describe Odisha the best are:

_____

_____

_____

_____

_____

My Odisha memories:

ANSWERS

page 9 LOST IN THE LAKE

page 11 FLAMINGO FANTASY

page 17 RHYME AWAY

Here are some words that rhyme with STRONG: dong, gong, long, pong, prong, song, tong, wrong

page 19 WHAT'S ODD

ROMAN, GREEK, FRENCH

page 21 WORD MATCH

Hello—Nomoscar; Thank you—Dhanyabad; Sorry—Khema koro; Please—Doyakaro; How are you?—Aapono kemiti achonti?; Goodbye—Bideyo

page 23 TRIBAL TWINS

A and C are exactly alike.

page 27 WHAT'S THE WORD?

1. D A L K H A I
2. K A R M A
3. R A N A P A
4. C H H A U
5. R E P T I L E

page 33 SPOT THE DIFFERENCE

page 37 HIDDEN WORDS

Here are some of the words you can form: abs, ant, ash, ban, bat, bin, bit, has, hat, his, hit, its, jab, nab, nib, sat, sin, tab, tan, tin, bait, bans, bash, bath, bias, shin, stab, than, thin, this

page 39 CRAZY CROSSWORD

1. D
2. H
3. G U M P H A
   I, I
   M, L
   L, L
4. M O N K S
   A, N
   N, N
6. M U S E U M
   S, D
   H
7. U D A Y A G I R I

page 43 TYRED

A and E are identical.

page 47 HEALTHY SALAD

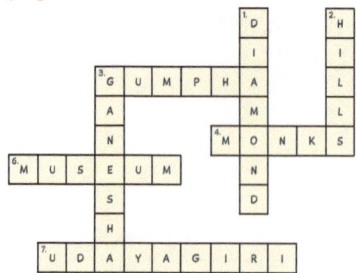

page 49 SOMETHING'S ODD

Gumboots, Cloak, Rubber band

page 53 MATCH THEM RIGHT

Padmini Rout—Chess player; Sanjukta Panigrahi—Odissi dancer; Jatin Das—Painter; Dr Ramakanta Panda—Heart surgeon